Fishing Stories from the Sprouting Pines Trout Camp

AuSable River, Grayling, Michigan

A Collection of Missives from the Director

By
Thomas R. Smith

Thomas R. Smith
yarnbody@frontier.com

Design and layout by Matt Faye
Editing and support by Ellie Smith, Dan Smith and Melissa Faye

ACKNOWLEDGEMENTS AND DEDICATION

My thanks to all those involved over the years, and those who encouraged me to tell this story, for making Trout Camp at Sprouting Pines a special tradition. From the early days to present, the memories abound. My thanks also to author Jack R. Westbrook for his advice and counsel. Going forward the stage is set for the younger generation to continue the legacy.

My special thanks to my daughter Melissa and her husband Matt for editing, formatting, and designing this book.

I dedicate this book to my family. To my parents, Woody and Connie, to my brother Sid and his family, to Ellie my wonderful wife of 52 years, to our special children Christine, Melissa (son-in-law Matt) and Dan (daughter-in-law Libby) and our very special grandchildren Nicole, Bethany, Thea, Monica, Eli, Cole and Grayson.

The most important things in life are family and good friends.

Woody and Connie

INTRODUCTION

Trout Camp, The Legacy

In the beginning, God created heaven and earth, Adam and Eve, fishing rods and Trout Camp in that order.

Trout Camp, on the main stream of the AuSable River near Grayling, Michigan, was conceived sometime during the winter months of 1951. The founder, my father, Woodward C. Smith (Woody), was then an administrator at Central Michigan College in Mt. Pleasant, Michigan. Woody and his wife, Connie, had two sons, me and my younger brother Sid, then eleven and nine years old, and an English Setter named Megs.

We were raised in this small Midwest college town in a big old house near the downtown area. Life was good. As kids with no TV in the early years, we were outside much of the day playing baseball, football, kick the can and the like. We fished and swam at the old mill pond, sledded down Borden's hill in the winter, skated at Island Park and walked to school and church. Curfew was when the sun went down, and no later.

As the story goes, Woody was walking across campus one day and ran into a professor friend who owned a cabin on the AuSable River. Woody said, "I understand you want to sell your cabin." The reply was yes. Woody said, "How much?" His friend answered. Woody took a chance and said, "I'll take it." Shortly after making the commitment, it occurred to Woody that he had not thought about how he was going to pay the tab. More importantly, he had not consulted his wife concerning this decision. Knowing in his heart that this was a place where his family would escape to nature and grow to love, he decided to confess his bold move to his wife.

Connie tells this story; Woody came home one night from fishing. He announced that he had done something without consulting me. I said, "So what's new." He told me that he had bought a cabin. When I walked in the first time, everything was a mess. I thought, "We are going to spend

1

more money here than we will in our home." I turned to him and said, "Well, I'll forgive you because of the beautiful fireplace and the quiet, serene flow of the river." Thus, the beginning of the great tradition.

Sid, Tom and Megs

The cabin is nestled in on the banks of the AuSable surrounded by towering pine trees. It features a large stone fireplace, natural knotty pine and cedar interior walls, old-fashioned log furniture, a screened-in porch and two hundred feet of frontage on both sides of the river. There is an outbuilding with hand-hewn log construction, which may have housed loggers during the turn of the twentieth century. This little piece of heaven was named "Sprouting Pines" by the Woody Smith Family. It is Trout Camp Headquarters and the hub of countless trout fishing adventures. We are blessed by having close access to the main stream, south, north and east branches of the AuSable River and the Manistee River.

After several years of camp governed by a board of directors, it was determined that it was a clumsy to ineffective method of leadership. At some point I, by default, grew into the title of "Director" which can mean anything from final decision maker about the good of the camp to seeing that we have enough creamer for the coffee.

I have written Trout Camp letters before opening day most years since then. The following pages reflect my musings over those years. The first Trout Camp, back in 1951, is best described in the letter written in April 2000.

The Sprouting Pines Legacy

Dear Fellow Anglers: April, 2000

On the eve of another trout opener, which ushers in the new millennium, I am compelled to reflect on the historic first official Trout Camp in 1951. Many moons have passed the horizon and fish have spawned the river, but Father Time does not change tradition nor the enormity of this event established by our forefathers.

My memories are vivid of that initial opening day. At the age of eleven, my younger brother and I awoke at three a.m. to the silence of the cabin occupied by sleeping fishermen. Unable to sleep in anticipation of the dawn, we roamed the cabin in search of the founding father. The only sounds were those attributed to last night's bean soup dinner (use your imagination). Unable to breathe, we took refuge outside to begin the preparation ritual.

First light arrived to the aroma of fresh brewed coffee and the sound of laughter as the fishermen awakened. Soon electrifying excitement and tension filled the air as they spoke with reverence of the magic of the hour. The mood was soon replaced by a deafening silence as each man went about the emotional task of mentally preparing for the oncoming challenge.

The dawn breaks. The temperature is 38 degrees. The forest is alive with the sounds of nature as the early morning sun glistens on the dew. The steam rises eerily from the AuSable. It's opening day.

Join us for the festivities.

Troup Camp Director

P.S. If you choose to fish, bring gloves to keep the ice off your line. If you choose to fish seriously, bring bait.

These were the days when it was not uncommon for eight fishermen to be back at the cabin with their limits (80 fish) by 8:00 a.m. The fish were pan fried in butter for breakfast, served with fried potatoes, bacon, sausage, and the like. Hardly enough food to survive the treacherous conditions.

As the years rolled on and the sons reached their teens and beyond, it was obvious that Trout Camp was here to stay. Soon marriages and children were a big part of our lives. The transition from bait fishing to fly only (catch and release) became more prominent. Handcrafted wooden riverboats and long floats into the night became commonplace. Grandchildren entered the picture, and so on.

The years have been good to us. It doesn't get any better than owning a cabin that is enjoyed by family, friends, old fraternity brothers, fisher persons, golfers, and others of all ages. Connie (now one hundred one years old) reminds me on a regular basis how gratifying it is to know that so many enjoy a place that she and Woody originated.

The following are other letters, or portions thereof, written over the years. They will tell the rest of the story.

Fraternity Brothers

April 7, 1989

Anglers,

Three score and eight years ago our forefathers brought forth on this state an event of great magnitude. Each spring, as we cast away the dormant blanket of winter, we are drawn to the vast wilds to partake in the adventures of trout fishing. Accompanied with this hazardous sport will be the comradery of friends and the building of fond memories. This prestigious weekend can only be attended by men possessing the highest fishing skills, character, and moral standards. For this reason, last year's camp was only attended by myself. Hopefully, more people will qualify this year.

The 38th Annual Trout Camp on the AuSable will begin sometime in the afternoon of Friday, April 28th and will terminate sometime on Sunday, April 30th. Bring your own sleeping bags, towels, etc. Food and lodging will be provided. Your father may come only if you want him around (your option).

The anticipation and excitement will build in the next few weeks. You should already be in physical training for survival purposes. Mentally and emotionally, you need to be at your peak. I am going up five days early to prepare.

Sincerely,

Director

Fathers and Sons

Young Guys

March 30, 1990

Anglers,

Thirty-nine years ago, I sat in front of this fireplace and looked out the front window of this rustic cabin at one of the world's most prestigious trout streams. Today I am in the same cabin with the same fireplace and as I view the mighty AuSable, my mind wanders back over the years. Many great fishermen have passed through these doors (and many not so great). If these walls could talk they would tell us of the wonderful friendships that were started and/or nurtured here and would recall the many good times which will be locked in our memories forever.

The 39th Annual Trout Camp on the AuSable will begin sometime in the afternoon of Friday, April 27th, and will terminate sometime on Sunday, April 29th. Bring your own sleeping bags, towels, etc. Food and lodging will be provided.

Your director has determined that the lack of fish caught last year (with the exception of those caught by non-sportsmen at Round River) was due to poor quality crawlers. Bill probably carried them around in his jeep two or three months before opening day. It is for this reason that all anglers 12 years and younger are asked to secure as many crawlers as possible prior to camp (you get the best ones after midnight and only if your dad goes with you).

FAMOUS QUOTE:

"If people concentrated on the really important things in life, there'd be a shortage of fishing poles."

- Doug Larson

Gentlemen, it won't be long. FIRE UP.

Sincerely,

Director

It should be noted that Round River is nothing more then a trout pond, just outside of Grayling, where fathers take their sons to catch fish so that father and son have something to take home to Mom to show that they really do fish. Sons are also coached before going home not to tell Mom everything that goes on at camp. It might cause unnecessary stress in her life.

FAMOUS QUOTE:

"What goes on in camp, stays in camp."

(source unknown)

Young campers at Round River

Kirk and Dan fishing the Main Stream

March 22, 1991

Anglers,

On this the 40th anniversary of Trout Camp, we reminisce back to the first annual event. On that occasion the quality and integrity of the sportsmen was to say the least, questionable. Judging from last year's experience, nothing has changed. Therefore, in honor of this prestigious event, the following criteria must be adhered to by all anglers:

1. All trout caught (except those from Round River) must be presented to the camp director for measure and weigh in. A $5.00 fee per man must be paid prior to opening morning. At the close of camp, ¼ of all monies collected will be awarded to the man with the biggest fish. ¼ will be awarded to the man catching the most fish and ½ will be given to the camp director because I'm writing this letter.

2. Claims of "The big one that got away" must be authenticated by a least one reputable witness and one 8 x 10 photo.

3. Some must report to the camp director prior to entering or leaving any trout stream in the county. Last year we received many written complaints from the DNR and other local fishermen concerning their tactics and behavior.

4. All anglers will be required to pass rigorous physical and mental tests prior to opening morning. Realizing that certain charter members are beyond the point of passing any minimum test, the requirements for these anglers will be passing 5th grade math and 2 or 3 sit-ups.

5. The camp director's judgement is beyond reproach. All decisions are final. Grievances, written or oral, are not tolerated.

6. Clean up details are made up solely at the camp director's discretion. (I'm not going to clean up that kitchen again after everyone leaves.)

7. The above criteria is non-negotiable.

The 40th Annual Trout Camp on the AuSable will begin sometime in the afternoon of Friday, April 26th and will terminate sometime on Sunday, April 28th. Bring your own sleeping bags, towels, etc. Food and lodging will be provided. Your father may come only if you want him around (your option).

Sincerely,

Director

March 22, 1993

Anglers,

As I reflect on the previous 41 infamous gatherings of great fishermen and anxiously await the demise of a long dormant season, I find myself on a new plateau of life. I am overwhelmed by the recent occasion of my kid brother, Sid's 50th Birthday and therefore feel compelled to express my most sincere inner feelings regarding the basic premise of our existence. Therefore, I have dedicated myself to many hours of grueling research as pertains to a fisherman's status in society. I have discovered the following (cannot remember the source):

In the Magna Carta signed by King John in 1215, it was recognized that fishermen (it was actively reserved for men at that time) occupied a special place at the right hand of the king (camp director). Later, in the Articles of Confederation drafted in 1777, in Article Four, the founding fathers provided that "if any person guilty of, or charged with treason, felony or other high misdemeanor in any state shall be delivered up and removed to the state having jurisdiction of his offense unless that person shall be engaged in the taking and pursuit of fish within the boundary waters of these United States."

As you can see, this is the first recognition that fishermen have a special status under our law. After the Whiskey Rebellion of 1804, all of the rebels were punished with the exception of fishermen, who were released on parole. This was in accordance with the terms of the Cod Peace of 1806.

Under the original Bill of Rights, the Second Amendment, which protects the right to keep and bear arms, had a second clause. The original Second Amendment read "A well regulated militia and fishing fleet, being necessary to the security and well-being of a free state, the right of the people to keep and bear arms and fishing tackle, shall not be infringed. Members of the militia and fishermen shall be exempt from civil process while engaged in their duties."

Unfortunately, references to fishermen were taken out in the second draft of the Bill of Rights. This so enraged delegates from the southern states that civil war nearly broke out 50 years early.

The answer then is that even though we recognize that fishermen are of superior intelligence and high moral fiber than ordinary citizens, they don't enjoy special rights under the Constitution.

Due to the foresight of our forefathers, we are privileged to enjoy this time, place, and grand event. We must never forget this historic significance. They have gone to the great Trout Camp in the sky.

Enough of this bologna. We need to focus on the old saying, "We are not here for a long time, we are just here for a good time."

The 42nd annual Trout Camp will commence on Friday, April 23, 1993 and will terminate sometime on Sunday, April 25, 1993. Bring your own sleeping bag, towels, etc. Food and lodging will be provided. As usual, you may bring your father if you wish.

See you on the 23rd ------ FIRE UP!

Director

March 29, 1994

Anglers,

Winter's harsh realities will soon be history and once again it will be time for the brave and steadfast to assault the treacherous waters of the AuSable in the quest of the elusive trout.

Due to the diligence of your camp director in the face of Michigan's most arduous winter, the homestead has endured. On several occasions it was necessary to leave hearth and home and brave the elements in order to pursue the tradition established by our forefathers. It took four trips to unthaw one pipe. It took two trips to purchase and install one mattress, and numerous trips to check for unforeseen emergencies. Twice, 4 to 6 men were needed and assisted in these endeavors. I am pleased to say that these all out efforts will guarantee the occurrence of this significant event.

Matt, Dan, Andrew, Trevor "Fun times"

While sitting by the fire one cold evening sipping my hot chocolate, I was overcome by the awesome responsibility I have undertaken. The question then occurred to me, "What does all this mean?" The following came to light. It was written by Robert Traver and is called, Testament of a Fisherman.

> I fish because I love to; because I love the environs where trout are found, which are invariably beautiful, and hate the environs where crowds of people are found, which are invariably ugly; because of all the television commercials, cocktail parties and assorted social posturing I thus escape; because, in a world where most men seem to spend their lives doing things they hate, my fishing is at once an endless source of delight and an act of small rebellion; because trout do not lie or cheat and cannot be bought or bribed or impressed by power, but respond only to quietude and humility and endless patience; because I suspect that men are going along this way for the last time, and I for one don't want to waste the trip; because mercifully there are no telephones on trout water because only in the woods can I find solitude without loneliness; because bourbon out of an old tin cup tastes better out there; because maybe someday I will catch a mermaid; and finally, not because I regard fishing as being so terribly important but because I suspect that so many of the other concerns of men are equally unimportant – and not nearly so much fun.

The 43rd Annual Trout Camp will commence on Friday, April 29th and will terminate sometime on Sunday, May 1st. 1994. Bring your own sleeping bags, towels, etc. Food and lodging will be provided. As usual you may bring your fathers if you wish.

Sincerely,

Director

Jack, Gavin, Scotty, Trevor "More fun times"

On one occasion after discovering that a new stove was needed, five or six campers descended on a store in a nearby town to make the purchase. The salesperson was overwhelmed by this crew but kept his cool while they counteroffered the price of each stove he presented. He made several trips to see his supervisor in an effort to make a deal. His patience grew thin. After what seemed like hours, the purchase was concluded. While leaving the store one camper commented to the poor guy, "By the way, you are out of popcorn." The salesperson was last seen slumped over in his chair in his office weeping openly.

April 4, 2002

Anglers,

We now move on with the great tradition of Trout Camp into the second one-half century. On Saturday, April 27th we will celebrate our 51st Anniversary.

I was at the cabin a week ago and was alarmed to see a foot of snow on the ground, the wood pile reduced to a minimum, and the cupboards bare of the food and nourishment necessary to make it through the weekend. Your director realized he had much to accomplish before the opener. The stress and pressure involved prior to an event of such consequence causes me to wonder why we do this.

I then sat down next to a roaring fire (toddy in hand) and struggled for the answers. It hit me like a bolt of lightening. We do it for the kill.

In the past ten years or so the popular theme for trout fishermen has been "Catch and Release." Portions of many streams are designated fly only – no kill (holy water). We strive to preserve the integrity of our beautiful rivers by giving back to nature these beloved trout.

While your director concurs somewhat with modern day thinking, I also believe that the fish were put there to be caught and devoured. For that reason I am declaring this year's event, "Slay and Filet Camp." Kill everything you catch until we have enough to feed the crew. Fill your waders with fish if necessary. Hand grenades are permissible. This is war.

Sincerely,

Director

April 6, 2003

Anglers,

The 52nd Annual Trout Camp will be Saturday, April 26, 2003. Your director will not apologize for the tardiness of this letter because he is the leader of one of the last official dictatorships in the world. I will write the letter when it moves me to do so.

Last year's effort on my part to encourage anglers to kill all fish for the purpose of a big meal failed because nobody caught any fish and if they did they did not disclose same (hard to believe). This year, the slaying of a single fish by every member is mandatory. The consequences of not doing so will be announced at a later time.

It has come to my attention that one member did not show up for camp last year because he was playing golf in Florida. This conduct is inexcusable. His name was immediately placed on the possible suspension list. Failure on his part to attend this year will result in permanent expulsion. The good news is that another bed will be available upstairs.

And finally, your director recently received a rather superficial letter from an upstart rookie camp to the west. It seems that they believe they own a place in Trout Camp tradition, and are making a feeble attempt to imitate our extraordinary history. I won't bother you with the contents of the letter other than to point out the following:

1. They seem to be unaware of the opening day of trout season because their camp is the first weekend in May.

2. The card game of the day at their camp is Poker. It seems fit because it is usually played by those of low moral character. Official Trout Camp on the other hand, partakes of Cribbage, a game which requires thought and demonstrates conviction and fortitude on the part of its participants.

While I admire their tenacity, I am saddened by their lack of experience. I am offering our training services to these neophytes in the hopes of upgrading the neighborhood.

Sincerely,

Director

Having said this, our poker games start around 10:00 p.m. and go until whenever.

March 25, 2004

Anglers,

The 53rd Annual Trout Camp will be Saturday, April 24, 2004.

I ventured north recently in an effort to analyze conditions prior to the opener. I was amazed by the amount of snow remaining, but humbled by the beauty of it all. The cabin and surrounding areas weathered well and will be ready for the annual onslaught. It was 53 degrees when I arrived at noon, and 20 degrees at 5:00 pm. I was forced to build a fire, pour a toddy, and sit back to enjoy this serene environment.

You probably all have noticed the large brown trout, which was mounted and placed on the mantle about two years ago by my son, Dan. I was present when this fish was caught. At first I was compelled to remain silent because of our blood relation. I now feel it is my duty as your director to speak the truth concerning those fateful few minutes on our beloved trout stream. The events took place as follows:

1. Steve and the director were anchored and wading on a bend where several large fish were feeding. It was the shank of the evening. We proceeded to cast into the dark mysterious waters.

2. Suddenly a boat guided (I use the term loosely) by my son, Dan, rounded the bend and encroached on our territory. Dan was steering with his right hand and wildly flailing a fishing rod owned by Steve with his left hand. A large wake was created.

3. As pure luck would have it, this monster trout engaged his fly and proceeded to the bottom, obviously unaware that it had been hooked.

4. An astute fisherman in my son's boat (Charlie) knowing it would be impossible for Dan to land the monster should it start to fight, leaped into the water and netted the fish. Total fight time was 6.3 seconds.

It is obvious to me that the credit for this fish belongs solely to Charlie. Now that you know the truth, please contact me with your opinion.

Dan and "Big Brown"

For the past two years I have strongly encouraged the slaying of fish for eating purposes. Last year, Joel rose at 5:30 a.m. on opening morning and nailed eight beautiful trout. He be the man. Most of the other campers rose at the crack of noon, piled in their cushy boats, indulged in spirits, smoked cigars, took naps, and came home empty handed. Another rough day on the river.

Sincerely,

Director

Joel and Brian

Many long floats in river boats are taken during the Hex hatch (hexagenia limbata) in June. Large trout feed on these big flies into the night. Food and beverages are a must.

On one occasion Bob the guide, myself and Vic embarked on a trip at about 2:00 p.m. on a warm summer day during the hatch. Fishing was good and the camaraderie was even better. Darkness came around 9:30 p.m. and the big fish started to feed. We engaged several (engaged does not mean you've got them in the boat). And we proceeded down the stream. At one point we were hung up on a log jam (sweeper) and the guide asked me to step into the water to push us off. With one leg in the boat and the other not touching bottom in the river I was struggling to survive. Vic in the front turned to me with something in his outstretched hand and said, "Do you want a cookie?" The guide laughed, I fell into the river and Vic ate the cookie. As the night wore on (about 1:00 a.m.) it occurred to me that our landing should be close. I asked the guide where we were. He responded, "I have no idea." My thought was, "This can't be good."

Cushy River Boat

If you miss your landing you must go to the next landing and walk back to pick up your vehicle and trailer at your original destination. Fortunately, we arrived at our landing and headed home. (Time 3:30 a.m.) Float trip, 13 ½ hours. We now call it, "the float from hell."

<hr>

Tom and Vic before float

After float – safe at last, 3:30 a.m.

April 8, 2005

Anglers,

The 54th Annual Trout Camp will be Saturday, April 30, 2005.

A fly-fishing legend and personal friend is gone. On Thursday, March 24th, Bob Smock Sr. passed away and left a void to all that truly love to fish the trout waters. Dan and I attended the funeral and were amazed at the outpouring of fishermen, friends and family. He truly touched many lives and his passing is particularly significant to Trout Camp as we know it today.

The following are thoughts from campers when hearing of his death.

Dan- "Last week on Thursday, March 24th we lost a great man. Bob Smock Sr. passed away and the fly fishing world (at least where I am from) is forever changed.

I attended his funeral today and was pleased that so many people were there to say good-bye to this great man. I suspect that the trout of the AuSable and Manistee rivers have one up on all of us this summer due to the fact that we will not be using Bob's flies in our relentless pursuit of them. If you have a fly or two of his I would suggest holding on to it. Life will not be the same without Bob around. As most of you know he was a great source of knowledge during the season. Hundreds of fishermen visited him throughout the summer because he always knew where the action was. Can you imagine dozens of fishermen wandering around aimlessly in Grayling not knowing where to go? Scary thought.

When I drove by his place today I was pleased to see he has headed back to the river. I am sure it feels good for him to be wading in the stream catching a trout again. I just hope he continues to tie up there because I know his patterns will be missed down here."

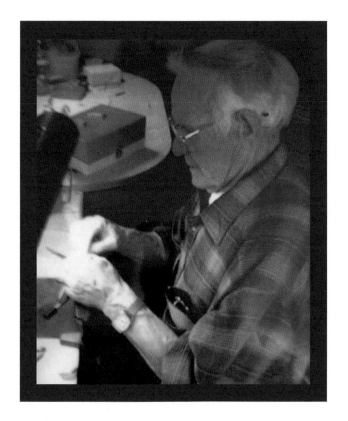

Bob Senior

Joel G- "He made you think how lucky you were to be a fisherman.
If it were not for Trout fishing, many would never have had
the pleasure of making Mr. Smock's acquaintance."

Joel H- "He was a truly extraordinary man in his own right, and a stop
in his shop was a must whenever in Grayling."

My personal memories range over a lifetime. I can still see my father,
Woody, and Bob sitting on the dock at the cabin during the Hex hatch.
They would drink a few "Cokes" and scan the treetops for the big flies.
Some things never change.

Bob leaves us with a favorite verse:

The River   (Author unknown)

Remember lazy summer days
Before the early autumn haze
Descends upon the river bed —
And signs of winter loom ahead.

Remember wading in our stream,
It's leafy banks so lush and green.
The frigid water seemed to make
It better than some tepid lake.

Remember how it used to be —
So pure and clear that we could see
The minnows, nibble at our feet,
In icy water, fresh and sweet.

Remember moss along the edge
Beneath the grasses and the sedge,
The river bottom filled with rocks,
Smooth stepping-stones for
coon & fox.

Remember pines that sway aloft,
Their whispering sound, so very soft
A clear bird call-a coyote's howl —
The lonely hooting of an owl.

It's still the same as you recall,
It's never, ever changed at all.
The woods-the streams-a dream come true.
The great AuSable waits for you.

"See you in the River" — Bob Smock Sr.

Bob was not able to fish the last few years. However, you can surmise by the sign on his shop door that he has headed back to the river. Closed-gone fishing.

Sincerely,

Director

Bob Senior

Bob Jr., The Guide

We have lost several campers over the years. With the good life comes happy times, but also sad times. They are sorely missed and are fondly remembered. Proof of a lasting friendship is demonstrated when after being apart for months or even years, you meet again and the conversation picks up where it left off. Life is precious, every day counts.

April 12, 2006

Anglers,

Once again your director sits in front of a roaring fire with toddy in hand and inspiration in his heart. Having retired just seven days ago, it is the first time I have been in this serene environment without work on my mind in 44 years. It's difficult to describe the feeling and although I don't intend to be idle, the peace of mind is overwhelming.

It also means that I have opened the 55th Annual Trout Camp three weeks prior to opening day (unprecedented). I will probably stay on for a while after you have gone back to work. It will be forever known as the World's Longest Trout Camp because it just may extend through the Hex hatch in June. Tough Duty!

The 54th Annual Trout Camp was blessed with your director's addition of the world-renowned fine cuisine master chef, Jack (Cozy), from West Yellowstone, Montana. Jack was kind enough to consent to traveling a long distance so that we might enjoy his marvelous menus. His presence demonstrates how prestigious Trout Camp has become. Jack not only prepared scrumptious meals, but also provided us with moral and spiritual guidance. He will return this year. Thanks also to Ron for providing Saturday night's Tenderloin. The thought was good, however, Jack referred to the meat as "street beef."

Gentlemen, here we go again. Camp opens Saturday, April 29, 2006.

Good Fishing,

Director

Woody – Original Chef

Chef Papa Don

Shopping for groceries is a pure delight. In the old days it took 4 or 5 campers and 4 or 5 grocery carts to complete the task. Since each camper might have a separate list, you can only imagine the chaos. Today's shopping is done exclusively by the chef with our assistance. (Mostly my brother when I can get away with it.) The chef might want to visit 2 or 3 other cities in northern Michigan to pick up specialty items. Shopping has become a daily event. But you know the old saying, "Do not upset the cook. If the soup is salty you say, 'The soup is salty, but that's the way I like it.'"

Old Guys with Chef "Cozy Cole" on right

April 8, 2007

Anglers,

Trout Camp headquarters survived another long winter. Your director was able to observe first hand any problems with freezing pipes etc. and therefore acted accordingly in his usual competent manner.

It was observed that several members went golfing on opening day last year. This behavior is not in keeping with Trout Camp tradition and is detrimental to our long-term goal of maintaining our status as number one trout camp in the USA and probably the world. We must focus on capturing the elusive trout species. Having said this, we will tee off at 1:00 p.m. on Saturday, April 28th. Join us if you desire.

I am sure that Trout Camp is close because Ron and our notorious chef Jack are already exchanging nasty barbs. Jack called and asked if I would call Ron and ask him if he would once again purchase the "street" beef for Saturday night's dinner. I contacted Ron and he said "tell him if he thinks his (Ron's) wonderful tenderloin is street beef that he (Jack) should go to Burger King and get it himself!" You can imagine what Jack said upon hearing this message. (The words are not fit for print.)

As usual mid to late June 2006 provided excellent fly fishing during the Hex hatch. Fishermen traveled many miles under horrendous conditions from headquarters to float the many streams available in the Grayling area. One fisherman (next door neighbor, Kirk) alerted your director to the whereabouts of a monster trout feeding after dark under the first highway bridge downstream from the cabin. Kirk said, "It's your fish if you want it. I won't wait long for action on your part." Several days passed and he warned me again, finally his patience wore thin. The next night we arrived back at the cabin about 2:00 a.m. There was a note on the door with a Hex Fly attached which read, "Monster brown trout slain, 23 inches, 3 to 4 pounds." The next day we confirmed the catch.

The truth is your director felt that it was about time that Kirk's camp had a fish over seven inches to brag about. Many years of frustration have hung heavy over their camp existence. Once again your director has helped the little guy on the road to greatness. We should be proud to be compassionate.

The rules of Trout Camp are:

1. Non existent

Remember this is a dictatorship, not a democracy.

Good Fishing. See you on April 27th!

Director

April 2, 2008

Anglers,

March Madness has returned. Once again the air is filled with ceaseless rhetoric from campers regarding meals, menus, and the like. Your director will rise above this babble and continue to provide cool, calculated leadership.

The old cabin was besieged with the long, cold winter, but survived and awaits the annual onslaught of good friends with various degrees of fishing skills. Your director continues to lead in this category. I do my own calculations and have determined that over the long haul I lead in all areas of excellence. Arguments to the contrary will not be heard or considered relevant.

The 58th Annual Trout Camp will be officially designated as the year of the Acquisition. My son and a friend were fortunate enough to be involved in the purchase of the infamous Ray's Canoe Livery and Fly Factory located near downtown Grayling. You will remember that Ray's is the starting point for the Annual Canoe Marathon from Grayling to Oscoda and a landmark for trout fishermen all over the country. We will be attending an open house for the new venture on Friday. Congratulations and Good Luck!

I have been told that only dry fly fishing gear will be available and only the most pristine holy water clients will be allowed in the shop. On opening morning, I will be sitting in my new director's chair on the dock at Ray's with a spinning rod, bobber (A/K/A strike indicator) and crawlers. The plan is to kill 8 or 10 barley legal trout and fry them for breakfast. Join me if you wish. So much for catch and release.

See you on the 25th,

Director

Woody starting the Annual Canoe Marathon
while serving as Chairman of Michigan Week in the 1950's

March 27, 2009

Anglers,

It's time for a change in location of Trout Camp. This year's long winter has driven your director to conclude that Florida is the perfect location for this 59th year prestigious event. By the time April 25th rolls around there will still be 4 feet of snow on the ground in Grayling. I have requested a Twenty Million Dollar Stimulus Package from the Feds stating that our presence alone in Florida would create a multitude of jobs and increase spending in the private sector. We all know the chef alone could raise the GDP by 4 or 5% in just 3 days. By the way, as your CEO, the director will give himself the twenty million as a bonus for outstanding leadership. So much for fantasies.

Director teaches son, Dan

This year's menu will be adjusted to reflect our economic times. You can expect burgers, brats, spam, canned beans, popcorn, oatmeal, frozen deep fried Cod (both Friday and Saturday nights), GI rations, mac and cheese, carrot sticks, cheap chips and dip, day old buns and bread, and the like. I found a deal on Pabst Blue Ribbon Beer ($3.00 a six pack including deposit). I bought 25 cases. You will have to drink it warm since we can't afford ice.

I feel compelled to discuss the fishing situation. Anglers over 50 years old are excused from fishing (optional). Those under 50 must fish. Not only are they required to fish, they must catch and kill at least one fish during the weekend. Legality and location are not issues. The species is not important. It could include, but not be limited to, Trout, Carp, Suckers, Pike, Rock Bass, Perch, Marlin, Shark, Chubs, etc. Your director will oversee the results. Penalties for failure will be severe. If we catch enough fish we could have fresh fish Saturday night instead of frozen Cod. As a footnote, all weapons other than fishing poles are permissible.

We also talked about the fishing legacy that continues to grow. Many of you younger guys now have children of your own. Someday they will hopefully be part of the Trout Camp tradition at Sprouting Pines. It doesn't get any better than that. Some of my fondest memories are those fishing with my children and grandchildren in and around Sprouting Pines. Great times!

In December, the director was once again blessed with a Grandchild. Dan now has a baby boy – Cole. During his first visit to Sprouting Pines, Cole was shocked to find there had been no planning in preparation for his arrival. Dan awoke to find him sitting in the director's chair contemplating a takeover. The good news – he let his parents stay the rest of the weekend. The bad news – there is no telling his future plans for the place.

Next Director Dan learned well

See you on the 25th,

Director

Cole – Future Director

In the letter of April 2010, I wrote: "It is with great sadness that I announce the demise of the infamous shag carpet. After gut wrenching months of deliberations, your director concluded that the 'shag' had served its time. I know this comes as harsh news to those campers who snuggled up to the shag in their sleeping bags on those long, cold nights (and days). The memories will live on. Your director saved some of the carpet. You may cut samples to place in your scrapbooks and take enough to install in a room at your home. Your wife will be delighted and you could use the room for sleeping if necessary. The shag has been replaced by a 'cushy' Berber carpet."

The shag carpet was a legend in and of itself. It was red, white, gold, green and blue and the envy of all who came to the cabin (slightly exaggerated). Like everything else including myself, it just got old.

March 3, 2011

Anglers,

The last Saturday in April 2011 will be the 61st time we have opened Trout Season at Sprouting Pines on the AuSable. The years have been filled with high expectations, low expectations, quality fishing, lousy fishing, no fishing, highly skilled fishermen, no skill fishermen, weekend weather from 70 degrees and sunny to 35 degrees and snow.

Many stories with various degrees of accuracy have been told and yarns spun over the years. These Hallowed Walls have witnessed laughter, tears, family, newborns, rookie antics, elderly wisdom, elderly antics, life long friends, soul mates and the like.

The long blistery cold winter has driven your director to Florida where I started this letter. The days are in the 80's and the nights around 60 degrees. Warm southerly breezes are common. Why would I leave this cushy paradise to once again assume the rigorous duties of Director? The pressure is enormous. Weeks of disciplined training will be necessary to cope with treacherous weather conditions, dangerous wildlife, irate chefs, late night card games, inept fishermen and sandbagging golf handicaps. The decision to return will weigh heavily on my mind in the next few days.

The next morning, I went to the Gulf to show my natural fishing skills. After about one hour of using every kind of bait known to man to no avail, I tried a deadly dry fly called a Yarnbody on my four weight fly rod and started casting. The other fishermen in the area were laughing and mocking my new approach. Within a couple hours I limited out on Red Snapper, Grouper, Sea Bass and Marlin. I also nailed a 34 inch Brown Trout. I was forced to leave early as the angry mob attempted to confiscate my Yarnbodys. It got ugly but I escaped intact.

March 15th – your director has returned to Michigan to assume his duties. Without my calm, collected leadership, chaos would ensue. I will be in camp the week of April 11th.

Opening Day is Saturday, April 30th.

Director

Father Sid

Son Steve

Father Matt, Son Eli

April 1, 2012

Anglers,

On March 3rd your director awoke at Sprouting Pines to discover 14 inches of heavy wet snow on the ground. The trees were heavy laden with large branches either down or drooping considerably. The driveway and parking area were cluttered with branches, fallen trees and debris. A large branch was hanging dangerously close to the power line. I immediately checked for food and drink supplies and was relieved to find that I was adequately stocked for a good period of time, especially with the latter. My thoughts ranged from "I am stuck here" to "so what." I might stay until the Hex Flies are here and gone. I drank two cups of coffee, called Consumers Power, and went back to bed.

I was awakened again by the sound of a truck in the driveway. My plow guy was here. He had blasted his way through the driveway. After the first two or three passes in the parking area, he high centered his truck on a snow bank. An hour later, with the help of his friend, he broke free and finished the job. Your director then took charge. Armed with saws, machetes and hand grenades, I attacked the still cluttered driveway. Three hours later, bruised and bleeding, I made it to the top. Once again, your director rose to the occasion, accepted the challenge, and won the battle. Camp was saved. I then drank two Bloody Marys and went back to bed.

I thought I had heard of every reason in the world to create a Men's Camp until the leader of another Trout Camp, Kirk, told me that they have a Salmon Camp on Big Creek in the fall. As you know, Big Creek is a small stream that flows into the North Branch, which flows into the main stream of the AuSable. It is then approximately 100 miles of river to Lake Huron where the salmon begin their journey. When I mentioned to Kirk that the salmon don't get upstream that far, he said, "I know, but if they ever do, we will be ready for them."

The Sprouting Pines Legacy

Anglers:

April 2010

In the beginning God created Heaven and Earth, Adam and E and Trout Camp in that order. This year we will cele Sprouting Pines on the banks of the mi

Last April I received an email from Tommy V. which I will share. It speaks well of our great tradition. It goes as follows:

> I was home alone, and received the Trout Camp
> Letter. I stuck my finger in the side and tore open the short
> end of the envelope. I touched the letter and then stopped,
> not something to be read in excitement and haste. It is a
> once a year occasion I thought and set it back down.
> I moved it to the butcher block top, made dinner around it,
> cleaned up the kitchen and house a bit and got the fireplace
> going. Checked my e-mails for the last time for the day, lest
> I have any distractions. I went back to the kitchen and set
> a tumbler next to the letter, filled it with ice and let my glass
> cool a bit. I opened up the cabinet above the refrigerator and
> looked at the Johnny Walker Red and the top shelf Oban.
> I chose the Oban, which is only for special occasions and
> poured one nip plus a little bonus amount. Since everything
> felt right, I picked up the envelope in my one hand and my
> scotch in the other and headed off to the couch. I took a
> sip and when all seemed right I pulled the letter from
> the envelope and heard The Director's voice in my head
> as I read…

It is now March 22, 2012. It is 87 degrees at the cabin. I predict hatches of all kinds for the April 28th opener. You must be physically and mentally prepared.

Trout Camp Director

As you can see from the comments above, the Trout Camp Letter in itself has become a significant part of the tradition. I am contacted by campers if the letter seems late. I also have been told by spouses that even though they are allowed to read the letter, it must first be opened and read by the camper.

In the March 2013 letter I wrote: Compliments of our hunting outfitter and friend Todd, we recently learned of a seven step program for getting spousal approval for hunting, fishing, and all other male excursions necessary for mental health. You might not see results overnight. If this falls into the wrong hands our world as we know it may end.

1. The first and most important step is to make sure your spouse realizes that you fully grasp the logistic complications that prevent you from doing this trip. Whenever it comes up, don't overplay the hand. Simply demonstrate acceptance and offer reasons to not go in a semi-melancholy manner!

2. If you are successful in this first and most important step, the threatening aspect of you leaving goes away and a softer, gentler and more caring companion should reveal herself!

3. Start to eliminate things from the to-do list for the time around the date of the trip. Plan ahead and do all you can to eliminate reasons that you have to be at work or at home during that specific time frame!

4. Let the topic settle and go about your every day as you normally would, with just a little cloud following you around. Be kind and considerate, but not obvious! As the cloud continues to follow you, look to her for the sun. It is very helpful to become dependent and needy. When possible, accompany her to Costco and be semi-bothersome and annoying while appearing to try to be helpful. Frequently bugging her for affection during this step can also be very useful!

5. The trip topic should be brought back up by her in no more than three weeks. If it is not, then you may have to find the right moment to intervene. This should be done at a time that your father has done something nice and has the favor of your spouse. (I recommend that you encourage this without implicating your father.) With no signs of an ulterior motive, think of how to get her to be inquisitive about the trip. I recommend that you retain the services of a nice bottle of wine and express your happiness that your father, brother, etc. get to do this trip together.

6. You will need to have your head about you at this point as this is crunch time! You'll need to analyze her inquisitive nature or lack thereof. If things go well, she might start to re-analyze the logistics of you and the trip. At this point it will be important that you offer simple problems which she will give simple solutions, avoid deal breakers! If there is a lack of interest, a motion to change the subject or things start to deteriorate, go immediately to her current favorite topic. The next morning review and consider Steps #1-3 and get ASAP to #4 and try harder this time!!!

7. Once #5 has been successful, ease up on #4 a little and SLOWLY start to warm up to the possibility of joining the trip. Only be semi-excited and gradually point out things that she WON'T HAVE TO WORRY ABOUT IF YOU ARE GONE. If she puts any pressure on you at this point to "JUST GO," cave and eat some Viagra. If she does not show signs of "JUST GO."
    Go again to #4 and eat more Viagra!

The 63rd Annual Trout Camp on the AuSable will begin on Friday, April 26th till Sunday, April 28th. Pre-camp for those 60 and older will begin Monday, April 15th and continue until we go home.

Director

Anglers

I am in front of a roaring fire again at Sprouting Pines. NCAA basketball is on the TV but Trout Camp is on my mind. I cannot guarantee that the snow will be gone five weeks from now but I can tell you that camp will prevail as usual. After 60 plus years, nothing will stand in our way.

I think about when Sid and I were young and the great times we had growing up here and fishing almost on a daily basis. We were a great family and the cabin gave us refuge from our busy lives back home in Mt. Pleasant. Now we can all enjoy the tradition passed down by Woody and Connie. Grandma is still living. No matter how many years go by, I still think about my Dad almost every day.

T'was a warm, bright summer afternoon in August 2011. Brother Sid, Guide Bob Smock and I embarked on a float trip from CCC Bridge to Three Mile Landing on the Manistee River. The guide suggested that a fishing contest was in order. We agreed. Since fishing is always better from the front of the boat, we flipped a coin to determine seating for the first half of the trip. The guide set the following point system to determine a winner at the end of the day.

1.	Landing a trout less then 12 inches	+4 points
2.	Landing a trout 12 inches or more	+10 points
3.	Missed strikes	-2 points
4.	Ordinary snags	-1 point
5.	Snags involving the guide climbing a tree	-5 points
6.	Hooking the guide	-10 points
7.	Losing a Yarnbody dry fly	-3 points
8.	Falling out of the boat	-10 points
9.	Losing an ordinary fish	-2 points
10.	Losing a big fish	-4 points

As you can see it was very possible that a fisherman might be in a negative ranking for much of the day. A short handled net was to be used and a landed trout was considered one that was close enough to the boat to be touched. The guide kept score and was the final decision maker for all disputes.

The trip started with Sid in front of the boat. The action was intense and the ceaseless chatter, laughter, and bickering added to the moment. My brother took an early lead as your director dropped into a negative ranking. At the halfway point, Sid was leading by about 20 points. He had no problem being quite vocal about his success. We switched seats. Your director decided to focus and soon rose to the occasion gaining momentum. Sid was losing points slowly and became agitated. He started flailing his rod in all directions missing trout, snagging up, and at one

point causing the guide to climb a tree to save his fly. I continued to gain points. With the lead in my favor, it suddenly occurred to me that if I stopped fishing and put my pole down, I could not lose points and my competition would self-destruct.

As we rounded the last bend before the landing, Sid was begging the guide to slow down so he could fish longer. I sat in the front with a beverage enjoying the afternoon and the lead. We landed. I captured about a 15 point victory. I was, as usual, humble in winning. Quietly shaking his hand, I congratulated him on a nice try, never bragging or becoming boisterous.
Use your imagination.

See you on Friday, April 25th.

Trout Camp Director

Tom, Fishing Contest Winner

Grumpy Sid after Fishing Contest

Sid sent me a text message after reading the letter which read, "Great letter. Full of lies. We will discuss the real story in front of Smock at camp." I replied, "No lies. Remember, the truth will always set you free." He responded, "I torpedoed myself. I am sick about it." Thus, the cleansing of the soul.

Illustration by Fred Behm

Woody, our founding father, passed away in 1974 at the age of 67. He was ambitious, fun loving, big hearted, and a friend to many. He could not have known the extent of happiness he would bring to so many lives. Thanks Dad. Love you.

There is no end to this story. The tradition will live on through our families and friends (young and old). The old stone fireplace has burned many cords of wood over the years and has witnessed the changes in our lives as time goes on. But for now when one is at the cabin, time stands still.

44716408R00033

Made in the USA
Charleston, SC
30 July 2015